Everyday Omens

Everyday Omens

Poems

Kris Whorton

Sheila-Na-Gig Editions

Cover art: iStock by ilyasov
Author Photo: Sarah Buckner

ISBN: 978-1-962405-67-6
Library of Congress Control Number: 2026934453

Sheila-Na-Gig Editions
Russell, KY
Hayley Mitchell Haugen, Editor
www.sheilanagigblog.com

Acknowledgments & Appreciation

To the journals that have published my work, thank you for providing space:

riverSedge: "Burn Pile"
The Jabberwock Review: "This Bright Moment"

I would first like to thank Hayley Mitchell Haugen, my publisher and editor, for her enthusiasm, kindness, and careful attention to my manuscript.

To Marcela Sulak, Pam Uschuk, KB Ballentine, Betty Whorton, and Linda Voychevhoski, I appreciate your careful reading and thoughtful comments. To the Two Sylvias retreats, Kelli Russell Agodon, Annette Spaulding-Convy, Jennifer K. Sweeney, and Traci Brimhall, thank you for your prompts and for your attention to my poems.

To Jessica Barksdale, thank you for your encouragement, companionship, and love through all the years of friendship and writing.

To Dana Shavin, Julie Roemer, Jenny Neves, Andrea Clausen, Sarah Blaser, Linda Voychehovski, and Mimi Jones Hedwig, thank you for keeping me accountable.

To my family and friends (near and far) and to those who inspired these poems, please forgive any misrepresentation. I am grateful to have you in my life.

And to Randy, who holds me tight and helps me make a beautiful life, thank you, always and forever.

For Randy, always

Contents

Part I

Part II

Part III

Part I

Before

I was a sunrise, a saffron colored crocus
emerging from the earth.

I was the delicate new green
of an ancient oak's spring leaf.

I was the smooth faded tan
of a chicken's egg.

I was night, the darkest time
before stars ease the hidden secrets.

I was a river-smoothed stone, red-brown
perfection, held in a pocket.

I was a dream as different from my parents' past
as the mountains they moved to,

the plains they left behind.
I was a jet trail expanding

against the beyond blue.
I was a third baby born, the last one.

A girl among boys.

Bread

My father's bread: a nightly weight.
Corn. Fat white. Wheat.
A push for peas. I sought
the gravy's dark embrace.
Shepherd's meat, we called it—
a lie I built on brown sauce,
salt-sweet comfort
to disguise the forced plate:
peas, canned cranberry, liver.

In college I worked in a French café,
devoured all the food:
Salade Niçoise, onion soup, croissants,
pâté, fromage.
And bread. Not my father's demand,
but air, heaven-scented,
from bakers who knew yeast,
fine flour and the whisper of France.

All winter, I planned a trip
to Paris, watched the bakers work
folding and shaping long baguettes.
Each morning, I ate a *petite déjeuner*:
two white quarters, butter, jam.
The crisp outside crackled,
crumbs mapped my route.
Months later in France,
sure-footed, I bought a loaf
in each neighborhood I visited.
My throat rolled out the rs
for *beurre, framboise, fromage.*
No longer a daughter or student,
there, I was a woman tasting possibility.
The yeasty scent in every crumb.

One day, I'd quit bread,
another tie to home.
But there, on those streets,
I wrote my own story
in flour and water—
shaped it with my own hands.

Summer of Twelve Showers

Prince Rupert, Juneau, Skagway.

We drove from Colorado ever northwest in a Volkswagen van,
took ferries when land ended, stopped at campgrounds, often
with showers. Never far enough from home to forget
I'd learned too much about my body from an older neighbor.

White Horse, Destruction Bay, William's Lake.

I fed the coins, soaped up quickly, washed the oil from my hair.
My body an otter's, slick with soap scum, mine but not mine.
The cold water couldn't clean me though I closed my eyes,
turned and scrubbed under the sad water spray.

Chicken, Seward, Talkeetna.

Each time my mother wanted a posed picture, I shrank.
My hair lank and dirty, unremarkable, never thick or pretty.
I grimaced, tried to be in front of a glacier, a lake,
on a picnic table bench in our campsite, in my own body
in front of the camera, that watchful eye that captured
a moment, held it long past the life I left behind.

Tanacross, Ninilchik, Homer.

But not past the sick hurt inside me, not past what I felt
being held too tightly, touched how and where I didn't want
to be touched. I tried to forget, counted the weeks, walked
shorelines, peered into tidal pools at worlds into which
I longed to disappear.

No Mailbox Here

On this sandy dead-end road
two empty houses from the sea
the internet and cell service are hazy.
No mail comes to the rented house.
You don't need postcards, or bills,
or glossy ads for sale items at Wal-mart.
You don't need Christmas cards or a quick note
from Aunt Lou. You don't visit home
like you should. Your old people are getting
more fearful, more certain the world
is falling apart. Inflation,
this so-called climate change,
missed opportunities to claim more land
from the polar bears and caribou.
They say we need the gas.

You don't want spiraling, toxic news,
so the T.V. remains a blank screen
reflecting you walking through the house.
From the windows, the deck,
it is enough to see the sea
waving onto the beach.

You stay away from the couple across
the road. Your first meeting friendly
but filled with questions about family
and why you don't spend Christmas
with them, a nudge as subtle as a spanking,
being grounded, disapproval about clothing,
boyfriends, every, any choice, and now
how far away you choose to live.
Low tide gives more land
so you can see
just how far *far enough* is.

Crow Without Murder

A crow watches us load rafts with coolers, bright
duffle bags, tuck away shiny pots, foil wrapped food.

Crows never forget a face, can hold a grudge. It perched
on the power lines outside Desolation as we hauled

what we'd need from our trucks to the river's edge.
At camp the first day, he tried to take a spoon, silver

flash against jet-black wings. We flapped our arms
to chase him off. He cocked his head, watched me

until the hair on my neck stood up. A hairbrush
disappeared from camp. The canyon wall's shadows

left at noon. We drifted down river, the crow
a sentinel in a tree every hour until late afternoon.

He made no effort to build a group or find a mate
while I traveled with mine, who I wished

to leave behind. On our fourth day, the crow
took a lighter to build a fire, to form a murder,

finally. I thought he would come back with others,
but he came alone, watched us from a cottonwood.

Two men in our group shook branches with dead leaves.
One threw the branch but never hit the bird, its black

feathered body a blind spot the man couldn't see around.
I left a ball of tin foil next to his tree that night,

an apology for humans with me and everywhere.
We woke to silence, the tinfoil gone;

the days that followed too quiet.

Mourning Light

Outside in the slant of light apricot soft
on rough hickory trunks, I clap for my boy dog
Swanson. His hearing and sight muffled,
he moves in a drift of dandelion fluff
and haze. A leaf falls from a chestnut oak
November brown as day breaks
over the ridge to the east.

I clap again, call his name.
The woods are quiet, sleeping still.
In the glow of morning, I imagine him
never coming back, recall my father's
words about his oldest dog seeking a place
to hide when her end days crept near.
He found her under an evergreen shrub
panting in the shade, and dropped to his belly
to retrieve her, then watched her
for weeks so he'd know
when she was ready though he wasn't
and wouldn't be.

Today isn't Swanson's day. He has months yet.
I hold this warm hope that feels in my heart
the way the weight of his head,
his contented sigh feels when he rests
against me. With the sunup now,
I squint for him. He is hard to see,
his coat the same mottled
red-brown of downed oak leaves.
I lose him at least once a week
when I fear he seeks a quiet place
and mourn him in this breathless,
waiting way.

A Garden Grows

The end was like the devil's backbone—
nobby and irritating as sneezeweed

stuck to my sweater. I wished it
had been like the beginning, growing

from a narrow throat to a full bell,
an Angel's trumpet. I remember his skin.

Soft as dew on a leaf.
His bleeding heart was too full,

too much pink and white to bear.
His bleeding heart embarrassed me.

Mine was always with the hens and chicks
picking around for worms or bugs,

scratching the ground for seed,
or root under the dead oak—branchless

reaching out but keeping close
what I needed to grow.

All That Drives Me

—after A. Papatya Bucak's "I Cannot Explain My Fear"

Fear of spiders hiding in my closet
or creeping on me as I sleep.
Fear of jumping off edges.
Fear of drowning. Fear
of what I can't see
in murky or deep water.
Fear of watching
a surfer drop on his first
skyscraper wave
not expecting him to stay
upright. Fear of a parasite
that makes mice
unafraid of cats. Fear
my husband will get hurt
or die or get hurt and want
to die. Fear of not wanting to die,
but not wanting to move through
each day anymore.
Fear of waiting when I should
be doing. Fear of doing
the wrong thing.
Fear of watching my father
waste away from his illness.
Fear he will stop
trying to live.
Fear he will try to live
too long. Fear of my mother's
future without him. Fear
of my mother alone.
Fear of making a wreath
of flowers for the dead.
Fear when I make flowers
into symbols of my own
meaning. Fear of losing
what I love.

How to Call in Sick From Another State

Tell your boyfriend you have a business trip
and let him take you to the airport.
He doesn't need to know you're meeting the man
who calls you every morning from Amsterdam.

The man, not a client, but a coworker
you barely knew before he left the country,
sometimes asks about software updates
or who's in trouble with the boss,
but mostly you talk about the slanting rain
in Holland, how the snow glints
outside your office window,
how you miss each other.

At the airport, call your boss.
You couldn't ask for vacation time
because you don't have any.
You couldn't call from home—
your boyfriend was there.
Let the boss' phone ring. Hope
the flight announcements stop
for that one-minute call.
Hope you get his voicemail.
And when you do,
say you're sick.

Board a plane to Chicago.
Three hours later, at the hotel,
step into the man's arms,
feel the way he takes you in,
makes your body quiver.
Let the fever take you under.

Every Monday Is Budapest

Not a day goes by without me planning a trip somewhere.
I scan international flights wishing for Rome, Paris, Lisbon,

Madrid to find a future home for when nothing can keep me
in my country. I'll take Helsinki or Oslo, Rejkavik, Siena.

Forty years ago, I moved to Florence to start my true life.
Language classes, a shared room with a German girl

and an apartment with two elderly Italian women. I ate
formaggio e pane, sipped my cappuccino each morning

and waited for the day to start, for something miraculous
to find me. On the walk to school, each day the same men—

road workers—whistled from their hole in the ground
where they fixed a problem made serious by their slowness.

At school, the coarse-haired Italian teacher asked to touch
my amber spun silk. Another teacher read from *Pinocchio,*

who capered and cried while I looked across the Arno,
imagining the valley view from Fiesole, dreamed

of taking a train to Vienna, Dubrovnik, St. Petersburg.
Each Monday my parents called. I told them stories

about my two signoras, new phrases I learned in school,
how the city was bigger than I imagined. While we talked,

I flipped through a magazine with pictures of Budapest
at sunrise, sunset, with castles, churches, a wide lazy river

like the Arno. I planned to never go home.

In the Family of Things

—after "Wild Geese" by Mary Oliver

Sunday morning, 1974

I would never be good, but I got down on my knees
and picked up the trash that I spilled across the kitchen floor,
although I said I didn't. I loved lying. The world was mine
when I made it up. My father watched, hands at his sides,
not on me. He never hit us.

But his gaze was turned to the window and the rain.
He longed for landscapes filled with great pine trees,
aspen groves, tumbles of stones and rivers, not one
with mortgages, and common things like middle children,
needy and sullen, who grow into womanhood
childless and distant.

Bird Soaring

My husband's whistle soars through the yard,
a purposeless tune that rises, swoops, trills,
the map I use to track his joy.
He greets the hens,
pulls English ivy from its roots,
waters the zinnias,
drifts from birdfeeder to feeder
filling them to overflowing.
He sits on a rock to study chickadees
and cardinals in flight. A goldfinch alights
on coral quince, a red-breasted woodpecker
picks insects from the sugar maple.

His mother says he stopped whistling
because it made his ex-wife rage.
I'll never complain.

I can't whistle and when he tries to teach me,
I manage only air and an occasional squeak
just like when my grandfather, the one
I loved, tried to teach me.
We'd fill the feeder outside his back door
and cardinals and robins
came close when they heard his call.
They kept us company in the kitchen
when he made us toast,
when he worked in his shop
and I sang to his tune.

My husband moves on into the woods,
his fluttering whistle takes wing
and I purse my lips
as though I'll blow him a kiss,
as though he'll hear my clear sound
born from heart and memory.

Winter Walk

On this January day, crisp and chill,
a snowflake's edge, no birds
cut the dove-colored sky, no lonely cow
lows. My dog pants softly at my side,
our breath made crystalline, tinkles
just beyond my hearing.

We pause, our feet sinking into snow,
to take in the gray distance as far
as I can see. The past,
my ended marriage,
and the future yet unknown
meet here
as the cold seeps
through my boots,
numbing me.

Closer, a fox arcs out of the weeds,
her flame-orange coat sleek,
her tail a bushy plume.
She sears the air,
ignites my soul.

When a Snowdrift Is a Wish

I'm dreaming of my father and blueberries.
As he eats them he says, *Blueberries are high*
in vitamin C and K. But be careful of the fiber.

I'm dreaming of Georgia O'Keeffe and a skull
over the desert. *It's just what's in my head,* she says.
Death and fecund flowers, smooth canyon contours.

I'm dreaming of following a kingfisher as I paddle
in a coffin down a river gorge. He flies ahead, calls
a rattling, wild message, *It's not too late to get away.*

I'm dreaming of a tornado swirling blueberries
in the air. Night falls. I cower in my closet. The moon
fades into silence against an ultramarine dawn.

I wake to a zebra standing on a coffin and my father
saying, *This snowdrift is a wish that keeps covering*
my fears. I shovel and shovel; the snow keeps falling.

While Picking Up Trash

Sunday is warm, budding while I pick up trash
in my neighborhood. Soda bottles,
Krystal slider wrappers,
a Wendy's drink cup and red straw,
plastic grocery bags
galore. More cigarette butts
than wood chips in the beds near the edge
of the grocery store parking lot
and spreading before me,
a black desert-scape,
treeless and cracked.
Bright sunlight makes me swear
for shade. But in the south in spring,
heat presses, a pile of quilts.

And there, behind the honeysuckle shrubs
a homeless camp. Clothes abandoned,
an old twin mattress, deck chair
cushions, a pillow. More food wrappers,
grocery bags. No one lives here
anymore, but I tell myself a story
about what brought them:
the death of a lover or child,
despair over a divorce, one too many
job losses. All things I've avoided,
except divorce which cured me
of my roaming.

I avert my eyes from the camp,
reach under the junk shrubs,
pull out deflated "Get Well"
and "Love You" balloons
limp as a cluster of dead flowers,
a Dasani bottle filled
with muddy water.

A blossomed bramble branch
arcing toward the sun
grabs my arm, makes me bleed.
In days my scratch will disappear.
In a month, berries will appear and ripen.
The cleaned wooded space will green.

A Wolf, Searching

When my older brother calls, he says,
Sister and I am 16 again. He is standing
in the cracked open doorway, the hall light
behind him bending, an intangible melody
between us. I am in trouble.
What is your problem? he asks.
I want to say, *I am a wolf searching*
for home. When he steps away,
I swear to the shadows shifting
behind him.

When my older brother calls, he says,
Are you coming out soon?
He is out west in our parents' yard
or his own, a man now in his 60s
and his words hold me the way I held him
when I was 8, my arms, tight, certain as a vise,
as he pedaled his bike hard to get us home.
Blood from my knife-cut finger spattered
his white T-shirt. Hummingbirds swarmed
the feeders at the back door
as we dodged
to get inside. My blood left a trail
the color of their throats,
one anyone could follow.

When my older brother calls, he says,
Come anytime. Green throated
hummingbirds buzz the feeders on my deck,
their wings impossible to see. Jays, chickadees,
wrens and redstarts soar from tree to tree
on my held breath.

Not just now, I say, gazing at knuckle-sized
tomatoes, golden globes outside my glass doors
lighting a path into my wilderness.

At the Edge

Beyond our house a landscape of edges:
tract homes, an empty lot, blacktop fading

into shoulder-high grass, a creek's whisper.
My brothers and I discovered a trailer,

abandoned, sky-blue-skinned, surrounded
by Russian olives green and silver sided.

The trailer's broken windows mirrors
of my own hollow wanting to be gathered close.

Held. Allowed to stay home with my mother.
Instead, we were sent into vastness. Each day

we visited the rusted shell, crept closer.
Its emptiness a language I was learning

to translate. No arms pulled me back
from the darkness I felt between grass and clouds.

A brother on each side, their hands in mine
the only certainty. Years later, houses

replaced the edges, the fields where we learned
the language of absence, learned to leave home.

Everyday Omens

Five golden planets and the moon.
A silver moon full against indigo
        slipping to ultramarine as dawn softens the sky.
A scatter of white feathers in the road.
Post-It notes a swirl of fallen leaves
        across my desk.
A faint scar around my middle finger,
        first knuckle. The fingertip skin once nearly flayed.
The buff and black stripes of a chipmunk's bushy tail
        left on a rock in my yard by a hawk.
A caginess when I see texts or voicemails, just before
        I open or listen and wonder what I've done
        or haven't done.
Tired white sheets on an unmade bed. Fat
        pillows flattened.
The natural bend of a red bud branch after the leaves
        have turned yellow and fallen off.
A fox's skull, mostly clean, atop the dirt as though dropped
        like a disregarded sock or careless comment.
My coop, invaded by a masked prowler.
        Three of my hens dead, but not eaten.
Abandoned brown oak leaves,
        potato cracklins on the forest floor.
Cold crisp dusk falls on my yard. The breeze bites,
        coaxes last leaves from the sunbright yellow maple.

Part II

At the Pulp Mill

The boom reverberates in my ears,
in my bones, beneath my tires.
I scan the sky for smoke
when we drive through early dawn
in north Georgia
past a pulp mill that somehow doesn't stink.
Its towers rise in the pink morning light,
steam rushes upward, toward the sun,
the full day, a shift change.

The mill's yard piled with pines stripped
of branches, of any proof they once lived.
Their ranges must be north,
the Appalachian foothills,
earth now gasping and wrecked,
like Lookout Mountain in photos from 1863
when Union soldiers razed the slopes
so they could see encroaching troops.

We're in enemy territory now.
All the trucks we passed earlier
end up here, or somewhere like this place,
looming out of the forest, clean and orderly,
where lives are taken, not by bullets or cannon fire,
but by the need for paper and pulp,
leaving behind a landscape, scarred
and silent as a battlefield.

Only the Stars

To live in space, I would have to learn more
about heavenly bodies—the sparkle of pinholes,
the hazy cloud of our galaxy, a luminous veil.
I know our sun is a star and Earth is not.
The rest is a mystery: how rockets or satellites
traverse the expanse, distances measured
in lightyears, why we yearn for the moon
or another planet we'll try to reshape into Earth,
instead of cherishing our home.

Others can go when it's time,
but I don't want to travel anywhere
that can't be measured in miles or kilometers.
I don't want to be suspended in a silent state
as I leave radiant Earth behind.
I refuse to learn a different planet's day
or traverse its barren gullies
lifeless and unknown. What if,
like when I scuba dive,
I use up my air too quickly?
I couldn't surface
in space, make it to safety
on some distant, red shore.

In space or on another world,
I wouldn't hear the *shin shin*
of corn snow falling, might never see
snow again, or our moon,
a crescent, full, or a ghostly memory.
I don't want to watch my planet
rotate from soundless space
as each continent passes before my eyes
and then is gone, a last fleeting glimpse
of all I've ever known.
I'd rather stay rooted on this Earth,
until I pass into mystery
with only the stars to guide me.

Beneath the Wings of Ravens

are fears we don't hold onto
but let dissipate—the crackling charge

of an upstairs argument, the smell
of hot brakes, the crunch of metal

on metal, the anvil hopelessness
of anyone unsure

where their next clean glass of water
will come from, if they can buy gas,

take their coughing child to the doctor,
pay their rent, sleep another night

and wake up to a world recognizable,
sure, without a nuclear plant

in a far-off land sending poison
into our air all the way to the exosphere

where the temperature is almost
absolute zero. But what of those ravens

soaring over ridge after ridge, their wings
black as coal seams, carrying the weight

of mountain memories? They circle
above weathered barns and kudzu-choked

train tracks that lead to abandoned mines
and devastated hilltops. Yet still they rise,

defiant as the people below, who cling
to this ancient land with roots as deep

as ginseng and hope as stubborn as clinging
mist and blue-hazed peaks at dawn.

It's Better Not to Share

The cold December blows in January
and there's no repenting or repeating

what you did. Forget the stolen earrings.

Your friend has long forgotten them.
Forget you stole from your mother's wallet.

She never cared enough to punish you.
The times you cheated on your ex?

It won't help to tell him now.

Don't tell your parents you only felt seen
when you were in trouble,

never in your early teenage years

after you visited your neighbor in secret
then never saw him again. Don't tell them

it took you twenty years to forgive

yourself, that you're mouth sore still
from holding your words.

Don't try to explain the system

that says women lie and men are victims,
the system that makes women scared,

keeps them quiet.

Too Much to Mourn

My red dog Swanson walks beside me through hazy
spirea blooms, sprays of daffodils, wild roses
of palest pink. Sun high in the clear sky
and he is young again, the pup I held in my hands
the moment his mother birthed and licked him
clean. From then until now he's been mine,
but those days are matchsticks in a nearly empty box.

My father's and younger brother's days are burning too.
Both sick and poisoning themselves
as we do when we want to live or feel we must.

I've read if we are lucky, we come back as dogs.
But I believe we die, a certain loss, the end.
This walking mourning is steadier than the seasons,
than a life spent speaking words, working,
being who we are in this garden, rose or aphid.

Shock Yellow as Sulphur

—after viewing Jennifer Packer's *Blessed Are Those Who Mourn*

A man on the couch, head on the armrest,
neck exposed to the world, is asleep
perhaps, but always listening to noises
inside his head, inside the room. To the stories
his mother, his grandmother, his uncle told.
To all the stories back to time and time before
as they converge in the shock yellow
home space walls, green leaves opening to Eden
in the corner. The pink square a blind, a soothing
block of color under brown fan blades spinning.
He is listening to the noises outside.

Is this the aftermath of death?
Is this apartment a murdered space with a man
too leveled to get up? When is enough
enough? When is yellow a hope-filled color?
Sunflowers. Sunshine. The yellow of butter,
of black-eyed Susans, of aspen or gingko
leaves. The yellow of the cloudless
sulphur butterfly, light as sun rays.
This yellow is the yellow of bile.

Time is the man's breath stirred by the fan,
by the respiration of the spear-leafed plant
growing skyward. Time dissolves in the room
in the spiral of movement and stillness
that is everywhere. Time unravels as it does
in any aftermath. Time is the sweep,
the spin of the ceiling fan.

High up on the wall, close to the ceiling,
a blue space. Inside that space, a bird.
Hope too high to see. On the ceiling,

a fat white bulb like a bubble, a great breath.
A sigh. Hope can live in pink cabinet fronts,
but not in the man in pale blue shorts,
the man alone with all that is toxic
and hopeful in this world.

At the Corner of Encroaching Birthday and Future Unknown

Cells dying, hair clumping in the shower,
skin slumping where it once stretched tight.

That conviction you hold that you control anything
as you plan your morning, your week, your life,

is not what it was. You schedule a trip to the coffee shop,
a stop at the store, you wend through town to the office,

teach a class. Each moment is at once that moment
and every other before it. This latest birthday

sits around your neck, a too tight collar. No one sings
from the mountaintop. The party, if there is one, ends

and you're back at the store putting oat milk and cilantro
in your cart, pushing it, yourself inexorably

toward the next latte, the next lecture on an ancient epic
no one in your class read, your next birthday a chapter

you wish would go unnoticed. The one you wish
you could skip along with the doldrum days of summer,

all conversations about politics and religion.

The Street Where I Lived Before My Divorce

Maybe it was the wide streets,
the boxy houses with contrasting trim,
every fifth one the same. I could see
too far in both directions
unhindered by mountain ash
or flowering dogwood shrubs,
summer's dry lawns.
The cotoneaster's orange berries
and hazard light red sumac were warnings
in October. Everything was dead in winter.

Mornings the house was empty. My husband
asleep at work or hauling to the hospital
a heart attack, diabetic coma, gunshot
wound, a staircase fall. Coffee in hand,
I looked out the window as the sun rose.
Expanse of grass, asphalt street. Sidewalk.
Neighbor's yard and squat
rust colored house. Above, the sky
a glistening azure. Cloudless.

At night, I stood in front of the window—
rooms dark behind me and waited
for the phone to ring, to hear the murmur
of my husband's voice, to hear
he was coming home. But in the silence,
an owl's heavy shadow over the moonlit field
behind our house, the press of aloneness,
all I had until I went to bed with only
space beside me.

Before him, and after, boyfriends
who filled so little of me
I needed two or three,
all who were nearly the same
and no different than the view
out my window.

Tinder Swipe

She is Madam Bovary looking for her dream man,
an escape from boredom, from a husband whose

voice is like a drill whining that the world
didn't give him gold, children she can't satisfy

despite working three jobs, feeding dogs,
cleaning a house never clean enough,

though she puts her shoes on the minute
she rolls out of bed, picks up dirty shirts,

jeans from the corners of rooms, sweeps up
piles of hair, forgotten toys, washes dishes

that should already be dry and away. Swiping
left right each night, she looks for a big dipper filled

with light, blackberries without seeds, for someone
to stroke her skin satin, lull her to a deepest sleep,

coax her awake the way a cloud of bees
alight on a daisy to find nectar. No one appeals.

Each image fills her with the dark of Lake Baikal,
that 5000-foot-deep Siberian beauty located inland

but with seals. Seals? How to find this kind of wonder.
How to find someone she feels she's known forever, one

to embrace while spinning infinities in the cold water.

A Dying Man Wants

When my father came home from the hospital,
he said the nurses were kind, cared for him so well.
He said they had fun, although he needed
constant monitoring, help
getting to the bathroom,
the assurance there wasn't smoke
or a squirrel
in his room.

When I asked him if he thought they'd be mean,
his gaze shifted. I watched his face
to see if he understood the words
behind my question,
to see if he understood
how dying changes living
and the living.

A week after his latest stay, I sat with him
as his doctor talked about treatment options,
said they could try this drug
combined with another.
That one alone. But nothing
would save him. Her eyes wide,
a doe's soft brown,
his a blue storm staring at his end,
then blinking away the surprise, the truth,
the longing to be held in caring hands,
to be cherished.

Country of Guns

In my university classroom,
a red phone is installed
a year before instructions follow
so I know who to call in the event
of an event. The phone is a wound
I can neither ignore nor look at.

A man with a rifle walks near my campus
in riot gear, but not one administrator
can tell faculty or students
what to do. I email my students, tell them
stay home or *seek out a safe place.*

If certain voters have their way
I'll be forced to carry a gun to class
come fall. More guns, they say,
equals less chaos. The math
doesn't add up.

I need options that are bigger
than Band-Aids or out-patient surgeries.
I need anyone who would rather talk,
listen, breathe, create safe havens,
than take lives.

Survivors

Two years ago, under the moon's
silver light, one of my parents' small dogs
was snatched from the yard
by silent talons, then dropped
and left for dead.
My mother sobbed as she told me.

When I was thirteen,
my friends and I snuck out
from a sleepover, chased each other
through July's shadows, swam
in a neighborhood pool.

Beyond the fence, a sedan rumbled,
headlights off. We thought we were safe
in our numbers, the five of us
laughing, sticking close to one another
as the sedan followed us home.
I shivered under the moon's crescent,
although it was summer.
My sixth sense itched
with a survivor's understanding
of how risky night can be.

When I visit my parents, hold
their remaining dog in my arms,
I listen for the thrum of fear
inside myself. I climb ladders,
haul out the too heavy trash can
so my parents won't fall.
I lock their doors
to the moonless night,
to the rumbling outside,
to the silence to come.

Among

Among the anthers of the lilies in my yard, bees
make much of the pink. Trumpet breasted,
fruity musk clinging to their legs, their throats taste
the powders, rich and purple-orange. Coated golden,
they blend in with the peeling leaves, moving
in contest, in a fresh circle, narrowing, ever.

I act as beekeeper, eye the garden well, caress
the speckled roses, dense and potent, an incandescent year.
It's open green here among the circle of bees. Rich sugars
burrow in my hives among the leaf-lightening trees.
The year's scents, fresh as grasses strum, like heart silk.

A garnet-throated hummingbird hovers over the stream
as I water. Blossom corollas drip. I hold my breath
to see if he will alight on the fall, tumble
to spreading sunrise lantana where water hits,
share nectar with this light so light.

Bird Speak

Sandpipers leave hieroglyphics of beak
and claw as they massacre crabs
emerging from their homes.

How do I decipher the symbols?

An eaglet shifts from foot to foot.
His talons leave pad prints,
shallow pits that belie his strength.

Somewhere a crow caws.

A colony of plovers and oystercatchers
race along the shoreline, leave a message
in the sand, a reverse braille I can't read.

Clouds press silence into me. The air is heavy.

I walk in expectation waiting for the crow
to flap overhead, rasp its wild call,
drop a single black feather for me

to scratch my own words in the sand.

Stumbling

My husband has started stumbling.
It's because of his shoes. Fat
wedge soled slippers he wears outside
to traverse moonscaped limestone formations
in our yard. I watch, silently spotting him
from the deck, holding my breath
until he makes it to safe ground.

Our fathers misjudge ladders, find ground
before they expect it, forget about steps
they've descended for thirty years;
mostly find, through error,
the clear path through a messy room.

Our mothers call, say, *Your father fell*
in the yard. On the stairs. In the bedroom.
Call him, they say. *Ask him how he is.*
Don't tell him I told you he fell.

Our mothers, certain as sunrise,
drive their men to the doctor's office,
know who to call to fix the car,
where to find the checkbook
or tea bags in the house.

I ask my husband to pick up his feet, wear
different shoes, pay attention.
I visit our mothers, skirt the edges.
Too much time away, sharp words
make me leery. Only when I see them
do I realize their fear is a mirror
of what I'm becoming.

When the Fox Speaks

When the fox speaks from the dry creek bed
behind my house, he's watching my chickens.
Any one will do, he tells me, *but the fat golden*
girls would be best. They're slower, more meat.
I'll make it quick. They won't feel a thing.
Of course, I don't believe him.

The sun's golden yellow touches the coop
where the chickens pace, pick at feed,
anything green. They cluck, sing their egg song,
call to me to let them free, but the fox is waiting,
somewhere amidst the tumble of boulders
in my yard. He whispers down the rocks,
to all the foxes that came before,
to the ones that will come to eat my chickens
when he leaves, to the ones that follow
silent trails winding around the mountain,
up and away to other prey, to clutches
of bird eggs, to the secret dark dens,
to the mates they seek.

I look for him each morning
in the sleek way he moves,
a ghost at dawn, a secret at dusk.
He watches from the shadows, says,
Don't forget me. His words
carried on the breeze
to my back door.

Orange, Found

Orange is the color behind my eyelids,
a tangerine glow pulsing when I close my eyes.

Sand dunes at sunrise, grains rough as regret
beneath my feet.

Valencia oranges, glowing peachy. A bowl
of dimpled, dappled suns whispering from distant shores.

My grandmother's hands stained
from canning peaches ripe with summer.

Apricot sunsets cooling in glass jars.

Monarch butterflies clustering on milkweed,
their wings tiny flames.

July's tiger lilies, spotted tongues licking
the humid air around me.

Touch-me-nots bursting open,
defiant against the drought.

Mangoes and papayas.

Sweet potatoes and squash simmering
spiced with cumin and thyme.

October's pumpkins, sweet gum leaves
pirouetting to earth, their dance bittersweet.

A terracotta pot where sunshot tomatoes
grow wild.

A rust-colored river stone worn smooth.

An orangutan's fur in a nature documentary.

Rare sapphires gleaming in a jeweler's window,
trapped in crystalline cages.

A bright flame.

A peeled clementine, its mist
sharp and sweet in the air.

The afterglow as dusk carries warmth
into the indigo night.

My bedroom walls—poppy and shadow—
where I always know I am home.

Burn Pile

It takes a few minutes and some hope
to light the burn pile
once I get the handheld torch and lighter working
and the kudzu branches free of the dirt, the dead
rosemary shrubs from this hard last winter
and brown leaves
from the hundred trees in our yard,
though they haven't dried
because the rain keeps coming.

The pile smokes
and I think of my father who hates
the smell of burning wood
or hates the way his eyes burn.
He would complain and I imagine
his brittle voice.

Earthy and essential, the smoke lifts into the air
and flames, just a flicker of light and heat
growing, burning
first the damp leaves as the fire builds,
then the branches
and logs as I poke and push,
create gaps for it to breathe.

Vanishing Line

My mother, in her studio,
paints a mountain scene:
bluish purple snow, a winding creek
reflecting spruce trees and sky.
Nothing about her art reminds me
of Pablo Picasso, who visited my French class
today, although he isn't French.

Picasso, the anti-Seurat, anti-Monet,
sometimes painted the ivory flesh of women,
like Manet, but grass never fluffed up
under his subjects. Nor my mother's.
She never paints humans,
is entranced by Western skies,
billowing storm clouds,
high country prairies winding into pines,
white snow foregrounds,
chilly vanishing points.

Picasso paced in front of the classroom,
grabbed a whiteboard marker,
and wrote: "From the redbreast
come memories." We waited,
even well-groomed Mr. Trumbo,
for the artist to explain his truth.
But he turned and left, his message
lingering like a half-finished painting,
a riddle in the air.

In my mother's landscapes,
memory seeps into each brushstroke,
a world both familiar and strange,
where white meets the horizon,
the past bleeds in
from a deep, inscrutable need.

This Bright Moment

with the young white pelican sleeping on the pier ends
when I learn north Florida has river otters

and I see one dead in the center of a two-laned road.
Trash, I think, at first. A tire? And nearly crash

into a marsh when I mistake the gas for the brake,
when I imagine what I would do to miss an otter

on the road. This wide flat landscape, this world
filled with people I will never understand

any more than I do the pull of the tides,
or the lure of blue sky and water, or the light

in this corner of the country where a dolphin fishes
close to shore and I see her eye, see into her golden life

as she herds redfish fry for her child or partner.
The otter is an unexpected creature in this land

of blinding brightness, stinging salty air.
This morning's shine glints off a white pelican's wing

and into me as I leave the otter in the rearview mirror,
carry its once living magic with me like a shield.

Part III

Night Journey

It's dark when we leave Chattanooga and drive
the two-lane road into Georgia. I watch for deer,
anxious they will leap from the hardwoods,
pines, high grasses, into my car or in front of it.

Do the headlights lure them? Shouldn't
the movement of air across the front of my car
push them away?

When I run along a road and a car
blows by me, the wind, displaced,
sends me into the trees, away from humans
who move too fast when inside
a two-thousand-pound Dodge, too slowly
down the center of a grocery store aisle,
stopping to think about watering the grass
when they get home, or remembering
to stop for gas as they place a box of Triscuits
in their cart, or offering an apology
for something said or a promise unkept.

It isn't until we are south of Lafayette,
near Summerville that the soft light of morning,
pink tinged and warm, signals the deer
to keep to the hardwoods
the way animals
who understand us better than we do
always should.

A Strange Relief

Let go the grandfather who snapped his fingers at you,
instead of asking for the salt or extra mashed potatoes
because you weren't worth words.

Let go his preference for your brother. Instead
of letting him see the hurt on your face, show him
a side of the moon anyone unremarkable might see.

Let go the father who tried to girl you with his words:
Stand up straight. Comb your hair. Don't walk so loudly
through the house. The father who thought any words
explaining a wrongdoing were simply an excuse.

You haven't seen a storm in his eyes in almost forty years
but let go the way it cut you. Fill your pockets
with apple blossoms. Make your own golden rules.

There's no need to be the bearer of quicksand grudges,
no sense in remembering. Let the memories fall away
from your body, mute as stones.

Why I Don't Go to Disneyland

Amusement parks make me sick.
Standing in lines with other hot
sweaty people. Kids jostling, whining,
pushing each other. On my first trip,
my brothers, our parents melted.
Sunshine and heat, still air.
Imagining how my dad agreed to a day
at an amusement park sends me
spinning and jerking in a plastic teacup,
free falling in a clackety
roller coaster car.

Many years later, my husband and I take
my stepson on a day too cold for resin logs
that float, bob, splash chlorine. The boy,
so thin, blue-lipped and pale
is wet as a seal. We stomp puddles.
Spun sugar and sticky cotton candy goo
smear his hands and face.
We stand under an awning,
eat popcorn too yellow,
so salty it makes our heads throb.

From that moment, we can go forward,
find the Haunted Mansion, It's a Small
World, the Pirates of the Caribbean.
We can still be a family when we're
together. But on this cold rainy day,
they head to the men's room to wash up
and I don't wait. I look for the nearest gate,
slip out like a thief, breathe deeply,
let the chill breeze lick my skin.

After the Funeral

The uncles and aunts, cousins, friends
laugh in the kitchen and living room

as they drink Hi-balls and great-uncle Bill says,
Come here, Squirt. He breathes his boozy breath

in my face, his meaty, sweaty hands on my leg.
The others laugh too and my eyes sting

as I slip out of his grasp, duck to avoid them all.
In the room where I sleep with my brothers,

I hide among the china cabinets with curved fronts
and old glass pockmarked like my great-uncle's cheeks,

as the sound of their voices rise and drop to a murmur.
When my mom, slender in her navy dress,

something Barbie would wear, finds me, I reach up,
wanting to touch her slicked-into-a-bun hair.

I want to be held, want her to explain
how my gramp's death is cause for celebration.

This will be the last time we're all together.
My great-uncles will sue for their sister's

inheritance. The lawyers will take everything.
I'll learn funerals are for families

to say good-bye to each other.

Navigation

Scientists say bats hear shapes: a spiral bounces, a square
smacks. You once heard a writer say plot has a shape
and imagined a parallelogram story, or a rhomboid, or an oval.
You thought this must be why your stories aren't published.
You don't hear shapes unless a splat is a dropped pumpkin.

Plants eat light. A scientist told you this. Not a botanist,
but a physicist who also said bees can dance a map
leading you to their favorite flowers. These discoveries
answer how light makes a plant grow, whether bees'
movements have meaning, what guides their navigation.

When you leave your house in Colorado,
you grab sunlight, run a zigzag on mountain trails
or in a circle around a boulder, and no scientist tells you
how to find yourself in a family that feels like a triangle,
why fathers make jokes about past boyfriends

long after they're gone. No scientist tells you
how to find the map to the shape where you belong,
the contours of a life that fit like a second skin,
the coordinates of a place called home.

Praying

I pray when I sit beside the slow-moving
creek, hear a hundred pebbles of moisture

drop from the trees. It's not rain,
but dew collected last night,

as the supermoon rose
fat and silver against the forest sky.

Blue jays argue in the treetops. A redstart
flits through emerald rhododendron leaves,

each one big enough to hide the slight bird.
Bigleaf magnolia leaves mottled green

and yellow will soon brown, die and drop,
falling with the birds heading south.

This space, wild, and holy, is home
to winter's juncos, crows, and chickadees.

Beneath that life, insects ravage the hemlocks,
immune to the trees' poison. Their branches

naked now, fine needles copper dead
cover the ground. These warmer winter

temperatures perfect for the adelgid,
not so for the hemlocks or migrating birds.

But the sky, by day, is soft,
dreamy through the dead branches,

the twig ends. By nightfall,
when I see the stars and moon glow,

I pray the hemlocks will green again.

Holes

Watching the heavens, I hold my breath
as the future opens above me. They promised
a hole in the ozone. I waited
for the sun to smash me into embers.
Scientists measure the ozone hole
from the South Pole
using weather balloons.

Do they find an old volcano?
My home? Anything white hot
against charred black wood?
My backyard pyre?
The fuel once lived and grew
toward that same sky I study
when I talk to my parents.

All we don't talk about—politics
and poor health—crackles
through the thousand plus miles
that separate us and a future spelled
in stars not words. My eyes
never burn until I hang up.
Time and space between us
is a soaring hawk
I'll never see up close.

When I run in the woods past a chestnut oak
that has lived for a hundred years
since losing its center,
it reaches ever upward
while I can't find my way
without my drumming heart,
my metronome
to guide me.

What is time but a broken animal?
A spell, a moon, a song?
Expensive, unspoken, not human,
not bamboo or darkness expanding.
I look up and around,
try to find the melody to fix it.

On the hillside behind my house,
two graves for two dogs
who died years apart
disappear beneath the leaf fall.
I'll add another this year.
His fur and muscle, tendons, and organs
will return to his parents
until he is nothing but dirt.
The hill will heal over the holes I made,
the ones I will make, the one I will become.

Orphan

With a mug of coffee in your hand, you walk
the perimeter of your mother's yard
as she tracks cacti pads for gnaw marks
from javelina or rabbits, peers close to blossoms,
checks if the watering system works.
You don't leave for a run until you've done this
or it will be the first of many missteps
you'll make during your visit.

Last night you left the window open, fell asleep
listening as coyotes yipped and howled,
first around midnight, again as the sun rose.
Those cries to each other, a family
unified as they called the wanderers
home, protected their territory.

One brother lives close, speaks little, words
too risky, too sharp. Your other brother
lives dead center in the county, split
between the main pack and you,
the outlier. You're not lonely, not lacking
anyone, only alone in the way you were
at ten, sixteen, twenty when you howled.
Your family never had a song
so you searched for a rhythm,
a territory of your own.

First Time Outside

The chick digs into my forearm
with her dinosaur claws, tilts her head sideways,

eye to the sky. She sees more than I can,
ultraviolet light, shades of this blue day,

the first in a week. A hawk screams. The chick
cowers, hears more than I can hear, how close

an enemy is, how that bird's call is different
from my soft words. Until my chicks reach

this feathered stage, they are fragile fluff.
Each time I seek them out, I worry

I'll find them dead under their heat lamp
in the garage. As they feather, I take them out

to learn the world they'll live in
where wire mesh and wood will keep them safe.

How heavy my heart feels as this chick blinks
lemony light. Life is unknowable, and I know this,

but the chick doesn't. How slow my blood flows
through my body as I try to disappear so she can feel

the space around her without me filling any of it.
She tips her head to study me, steps to my hand,

sits, her heat warm in my palm. I wonder at her trust
then realize she doesn't know not to trust.

She knows gentle touch, electric fear.
The way living things are hardwired to know

when to run away, when to hide,
when to let the shadow of a larger creature

protect us when we turn our face up for the sun's kiss.

Saturn Up Close

With one eye closed, the other pressed
to the tiny telescope lens, you see
an orange glow, a brightness and color
so unexpected and huge
you pull back, look up at
the spot that is Saturn
right in front of you.

Ninety-five times more massive than earth,
you still see the ghost of Saturn's glow
in the starlit night, so close
but you cannot touch it.
Its perfect beauty shocks too much
for you to look through that eyepiece
again, to see those arcing rings,
like wedding bands,
like some other lifetime,
like shackles holding you to a future
that takes the ground out
from under you.

A crisp chime should sound to break
the utter quiet of this place,
set the surprise of the sight
against this above timberline world,
blackness all around.
But there is only silence
aside from your breathing
and the shackles are welcome.
They hold you to this place. This earth.

When My Mother Calls Crying

I hear the cracked way she says my name
as though she's dropped an egg and its center

is spilling out. *Phonic dysphonia* the doctor said
to explain the wavering break of her words;

he told her to sing to remind her vocal cords
they were once flexible. But she won't sing,

this mother from whom I learned not to sing.
This mother who taught me to paint, to plant,

to nurture by being present. In the space
between her words is what she doesn't say

about me taking my younger brother to chemo.
I watch the nurse press needles

into his abdomen, watch him fall asleep
when the Benadryl takes hold. In that space

lives her regret for not leaving her desert home
to see her youngest, not caring for him

through aging and illness, his and hers.
A vise constricts her throat, squeezes the cords,

holds back her words, the ones she might
shape as carefully as a memory.

Or she might not say a thing and I remember
how we used to exchange letters

when we couldn't talk to one another
because the words were too hard to press

out of our mouths, too hot, unsingable.
They come too late to make absence right.

The Meaning of Truffles

Outside Assisi, Michele, his Pointer and I hunt
for truffles in sun-baked hills.
Lemony light filters through oak leaves
as we wade through high grass.

The dog sniffs, paws. Michele kneels.
Silver blade in hand, he eases a truffle from earth—
black, wrinkled as an old walnut casing
holding darkness and delicious secrets.

Years ago, when I was in high school,
my older boyfriend bought chocolate truffles,
man-made delights
filled with champagne and cream.

In a comped hotel room where he worked,
we stripped, ate the truffles in bed. Sweet
on my tongue, a smear on my skin.
I told no one, hoped he'd trust me for a while.

His jealousy crowded me like his jeep
parked across the street from my school.
Too possessive, his words, his truffle gifts
tasted chalky, stale in my mouth.

When I ended it, he left flowers with a note
I refused to read. Now, as the Italian sun
climbs high, I return to Perugia
with once earth-bound truffles,

grate them onto fresh asparagus and pasta.
Later, I'll buy chocolate in the sun-warmed city,
savor the difference between sweetness
and the earthy tang of freedom.

My Brother's World

He speaks into an imaginary mic on his wrist
and tells me his twin Alan is wearing a red shirt.
He doesn't have a twin; when I explain
that his full name is Michael Alan, he insists
it's his birthday and our server will bring
chocolate cake with ice cream. It's February.
His birthday is in November and there's no
convincing him I'm right.

When we were kids, we played in open fields,
forested trails, the school playground near our house.
We searched for caves, caught water skippers in creeks.
Gentle, sweet, Down's syndrome made him different.
I didn't know to wonder why and mostly worried
I would get in trouble if I didn't keep him safe.

We wait for his chemo treatment for leukemia.
Out the window, patches of snow dot
the foothills we grew up exploring.
Michael tells me what he was wearing
when my husband and I met over 30 years ago
and it was his birthday. I don't remember
if he's right, but tell him again
it wasn't his birthday as I wonder why
I can't let everyday be his birthday.

This day is close to ending, the low clouds heavy.
My brother says my name; when I turn, he calls me
Gray hair, says, *You had brown hair once.*

Out There, Somewhere

I wish there was an app to help me understand space,
its emptiness, soundlessness and blackness complete.
I'd close my eyes and reopen them and know
all there is to know
not only in my brain but also in my heart,
a blooming great red dahlia.

To know the location of airy gaseous clusters
and drifts sent by the Webb telescope,
I need to know galaxies,
quadrants, lightyears, a way to travel to the worlds
that appear in my inbox, to that world
that is a deep purple centered orchid with violet petals
lit from behind, from within by white and yellow stars.

When I look into the black beyond, I don't see
an escape option from this planet we're slowly suffocating.
I see a loss of shadows dappling green under the redbuds
when they speak to the air, a dawn that comes on
so softly peach it makes the morning ache,
a red fox hunting in my yard
instead of the woods amongst the sticks
dowsers use.

Here and known, this sky
reaches through sunlight
to sugar maples, chestnut oak,
dogwoods to clouds
puffing free.

Bittersweet

My mother had dried stalks with small orange berries
in a sterling silver vase that was her grandmother's.

Bittersweet, she called it. Did she feel that way
when she looked at the vase? Her grandmother grew the plant,

said the berry was a sunset. Her grandmother was sent
to the state hospital when she couldn't find her home,

couldn't remember her husband, remember to dress
before she went outside. The branches were covered

with clusters of red-orange fruit winged
by silvery seed coats. Down the street from my home,

bittersweet sprawls over bushes and fences, spreads
across the ground. I call my mother, tell her

I remember the vase with the delicate gems,
discovered the brilliant berries after many years

of not seeing them. I describe their perfect smoothness,
the creeping plant they grow on, one I've seen

hundreds of times but never seen. I ask her to tell me
about her grandmother, to remember the woman she loved.

I ask my mother to remember her memories.

When the Tomatoes Come In

This summer the vines are heavy. Clusters
of fat-as-limes tomatoes cover the shrubs.
I walk the paths between plants
imagining great harvests.

July is hot, early August hotter still.
It's dry enough for the hickory to drop
lanceolate leaves before summer is half over.
Every leaf hangs limp as socks on a clothesline.

The tomatoes stay green. I watch and water,
check for signs of orange or red, faint
as a faraway taillight in fog. I pick
dead leaves off, pinch new starts,
pat the green fruit with my fingers.

Every year until this one
I've left my home in summer,
spent time in my old western life
or gone abroad.

This year my old dog Swanson's days are filled
with more hours of sleep than play.
One day soon he'll let me know he's ready,
so I stay close to him, walk the paths,
and peer at the tomatoes.

I water morning and evening
as the sun drops behind the mountain.
I'm open to the start of color.

Such Quiet

In the hospital room, your father is in the bed, dozing.
Tubes run from machines to his nose, to a needle
stuck deep into his hand. When you were young,

he spoke only on the full moon, when your family
cross-country skied, when he helped you with math,
your least good subject. Now he is chatty.

Your mother sits close, crocheting. She watches
the carmine yarn take shape into lace.
The hook smooth and sure in her right hand,

the one she used to show you how to tap cinnamon
from a spice jar, turn a squeeze of deep green paint
into a tree on rag paper, pinch an unwanted bud

to make tomato plants and roses thrive. Her silence
complete, not the softness of sound when cotton balls
plug your ears, not the white cold aloofness

of your teenage years, but of a mother not yours.
Inside her head she holds the image of the pattern
she's using, counting chain or slip-stitch,

bobble or cluster, the ingredients for cranberry relish
and German potato salad, recipes her mother used,
the obscure genealogy of names, kinship old

and unknown to anyone still living. Counting,
through each minute, the future is too heavy to lift,
she's too weighed down to stand. She might lay her hand

on your father's thin hair, stroke his wrinkled forehead.
Outside the desert is the brushy green of paloverde
and mesquite, of cacti, sharp and dry.

If she grabs her purse, walks out, rushes away
from the words the doctors or nurses might say,
she has time. Quiet and alone takes practice.

How to Practice Augury

Starlings and their smoke cloud murmurations
are the surest sign the symphonies unfurl above us.
A crow's call foretells calamity, a dove's peace.
This is what the ancients said. As a child, I didn't
watch birds or listen to their songs and only noticed robins
picking fat worms from the lawn. I dismissed
all birds as simply birds, as though nothing
could be learned from a young dead one in the road,
as though birds had no urge to push their offspring
forward, no wish to see them fly in air as clean
sparkling as the dreams they held.

Years later I watched the flick of bluebirds
when they lifted off reeds. Kestrels
and red-tailed hawks soared big skies,
blue jays and magpies badgered campers
for food, scrounged carcasses along a trail.
Bald eagles were rare until I saw a hundred or more
perched along the Chilkat River in Alaska.
They waited, keen eyes on the water as fat
red backed salmon fought the current
before they were carried into the sky.
Each feather I found after that
was worth consideration.

From the hospital window, while my father
has blood drawn, I spot black-headed vultures
in relief against the sky. I used to watch them circle
overhead and wonder at the death they sought
until I learned they are symbols of protection.
Grace as they soar high above scruffy desert,
comfort in their shadows on the ground.

About the Author

Kris Whorton is the author of the poetry collection *Alchemy* (2023). Originally from Boulder, Colorado, she has lived in the South since 1997. She teaches creative, scientific, and professional writing at the University of Tennessee at Chattanooga, where she also served as assistant director of the Meacham Writers' Workshop. Her poems, fiction, and creative nonfiction have appeared in journals and anthologies. Whorton holds an MFA in Creative Writing from the Rainer Writing Workshop and has worked with teens, adults, and incarcerated writers in Hamilton and Bradley County Jails. She lives in the woods with her husband and two Australian shepherds.

S
Sheila-Na-Gig Editions

www.ingramcontent.com/pod-product-compliance
Ingram Content Group UK Ltd.
Pitfield, Milton Keynes, MK11 3LW, UK
UKHW042012190726
13854UKWH00005B/2263